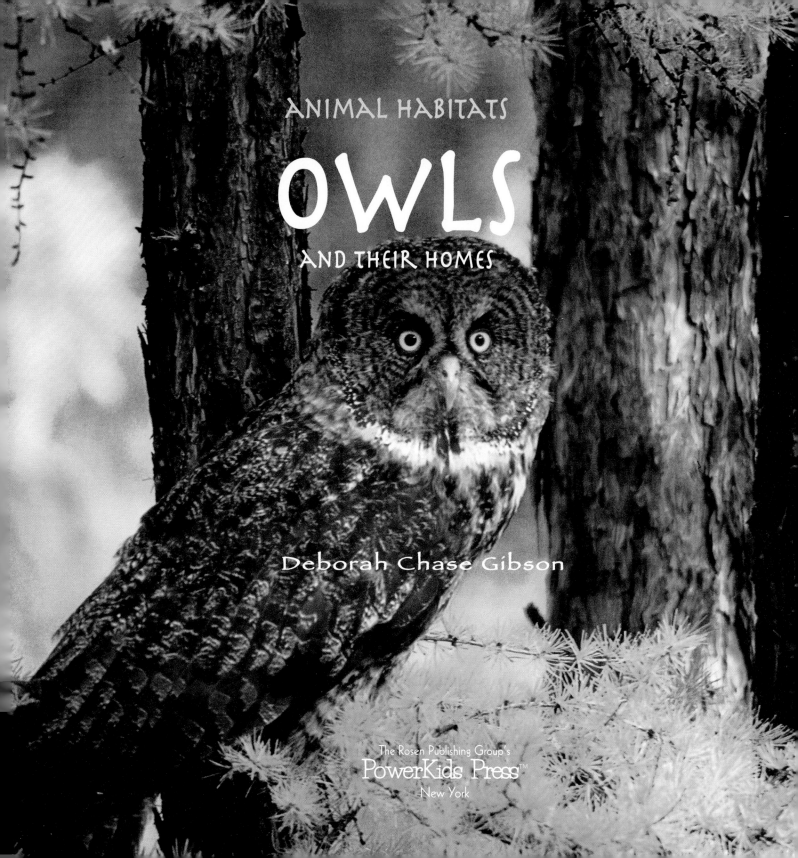

ANIMAL HABITATS

OWLS

AND THEIR HOMES

Deborah Chase Gibson

The Rosen Publishing Group's
PowerKids Press™
New York

Published in 1999 by The Rosen Publishing Group, Inc.
29 East 21st Street, New York, NY 10010

First Edition

Book Design: Kim Sonsky

Photo Credits: Cover, title page, pp. 3, 17 © FPG/Gail Shumway; p. 5 © International Stock/Dusty Willison; p. 6 © FPG/Lee Kuhn; p. 7 © Animals Animals/Leach OSF; pp. 8, 9, 18 © International Stock/Bob Jacobson; p. 10 © 1996 PhotoDisc, Inc.; p. 13 © Animals Animals/Richard Kolar; p. 14 © Animals Animals/Ted Levin; p. 15 © Animals Animals/Paul Berquist; p. 16 © Animals Animals/Steven David Miller; p. 19 © FPG/Leonard Lee Rue; pp. 20, 22 © Animals Animals/Bill Beatty; p. 21 © Animals Animals/John Gerlach.

Gibson, Deborah Chase.
    Owls and their homes / by Deborah Chase Gibson.
        p.   cm. — (Animal Habitats)
    Includes index.
    Summary: Presents an overview of different kinds of owls and how and where they make their homes.
    ISBN 0-8239-5308-4
    1. Owls—Juvenile literature. 2. Owls—Habitat—Juvenile literature. [1. Owls.] I. Title. II. Series: Gibson, Deborah Chase.
    Animal habitats.
    QL696.S8G535 1998
    598.9'7–dc21   98-15375
                                                                                               CIP
                                                                                                AC

Manufactured in the United States of America

CONTENTS

1 Owls of the World   4
2 What Are Owls Like?   6
3 The Barn Owl   8
4 The Arctic   11
5 The Snowy Owl   12
6 Desert Owls   15
7 Burrowing Owls   16
8 The Great Horned Owl   19
9 Baby Owls   20
10 Owls and Humans   22
   Web Sites   22
   Glossary   23
   Index   24

OWLS OF THE WORLD

There are over 130 **species** (SPEE-sheez), or kinds, of owls. Owls can be found in all parts of the world except Antarctica. North America alone is home to nineteen different species of owls.

Owls are found in many different **habitats** (HA-bih-tats), such as deserts, forests, **prairies** (PRAYR-eez) and even the Arctic **tundra** (TUN-druh). They nest in trees, in holes in the ground, in barns, and in caves. And while many other birds **migrate** (MY-grayt) to warmer places during the winter, most owls do not. They live in the same place all year round.

The barred owl can be found in warm places, such as the Everglades in Florida. ▶

WHAT ARE OWLS LIKE?

Even though they can't see colors, owls see much better than people do. Good eyesight is helpful to owls because they are **nocturnal** (nok-TER-nul). That means they are most active at night when there isn't much light.

Owls have sharp claws called **talons** (TA-lunz), which they use to capture and kill **prey** (PRAY), such as mice, rats, and snakes. Owls aren't very good at building their own nests, so they use nests left by other birds, such as hawks. Owls also like to live in human-made places, like barns or old buildings.

The sharp talons of a barn owl help it catch and
carry small prey easily.

THE BARN OWL

Barn owls live all over the world. They are known for their large, dark eyes that peek out of feathered, heart-shaped faces.

Just like the name says, barn owls like to live in barns. Old buildings and hollow trees also make good nesting spots for these owls. In the United States, you can find barn owls in the southern and middle states from coast to coast.

Farmers like to have barn owls around because barn owls kill and eat **rodents** (ROH-dents), including mice and rats.

Barn owls prey on rodents that might eat food meant for farm animals, such as cows and horses. ▶

THE ARCTIC

The very northern parts of Alaska, Canada, Europe, and Siberia lie in and near the cold, icy Arctic Circle. The land in the Arctic is called tundra. It is so cold in this part of the world that the top six inches of the land is frozen solid all year round.

Although it is very cold, there is life on the tundra. Moss, flowers, and other plants grow during the short summer. The tundra also has many summer visitors, such as migrating caribou and geese.

Polar bears, seals, and whales also live in this cold **climate** (KLY-mit). Snowy owls live there too.

◀ The snowy owl shares its tundra habitat with other Arctic creatures, such as the polar bear.

THE SNOWY OWL

Snowy owls blend in well with the icy Arctic. Their white feathers are sprinkled with small black or brown spots. This **camouflage** (KA-muh-flaj) makes it hard for the snowy owls' **predators** (PREH-duh-terz) to see them. It also helps snowy owls sneak up on their prey.

Snowy owls make their nests in places where they can easily see predators and prey. Big rocks or small hills on the treeless tundra are common nesting places.

Snowy owls grow to be about twenty inches tall. Small rodents called lemmings are the snowy owl's favorite meal.

There aren't any trees on the tundra, so the snowy owl's nest is really just a shallow hole in the snow and ice. ▶

The elf owl is one of the smallest owls in the world. Another tiny owl is the saw-whet owl, who shares its habitat with the elf owl. ▶

◀ The screech owl, another kind of desert owl, also likes to make its nest in cactuses.

DESERT OWLS

Owls live in deserts too. At just six inches long, elf owls are one of the smallest owls in the world. These owls make their homes in the warm climate of the southwestern United States and Mexico.

One of the elf owl's favorite places to nest is in the giant **saguaro** (suh-GWAR-oh) cactus. Elf owls often nest inside holes in the plant. A popular **perch** (PERCH) is where the limbs of the saguaro meet the main stem of the cactus. If they can't find a cactus, elf owls will live in woodpecker holes in trees or in plants on the desert floor.

BURROWING OWLS

Some owls make their homes right in the ground. **Burrowing** (BUR-oh-ing) owls find empty holes and tunnels that were dug out by other animals. Gopher and prairie-dog nests are good places for burrowing owls to make their homes. If they can't find any empty nests, these long-legged owls dig their own.

Burrowing owls live on the open grasslands of North, Central, and South America. Their feathers are usually brown with white spots.

Other owls don't share their nests, but burrowing owls will share their winter homes with each other.

Burrowing owls will often live in empty prairie-dog burrows. ▶

16

THE GREAT HORNED OWL

Great horned owls are found in cold forests in Alaska, in hot deserts in the southwestern United States, and in warm, tropical **rain forests** (RAYN FOR-ests) in South America.

These grayish and white-spotted owls are among the largest owls on Earth. They can grow up to two feet long. The clusters of feathers that stick out of their heads give the great horned owl their name.

These fierce predators like to find nests that other large birds, such as hawks, have left. A pair of great horned owls use the nest to raise their babies, called owlets.

◀ Great horned owls have wingspans of four to five feet.

19

BABY OWLS

When great horned owls **mate** (MAYT), they can have about two babies a year. The female lays her eggs in the winter, one at a time and a few days apart. While she sits on her eggs in the nest to keep them warm, the male hunts for food. He brings food to the female so she doesn't have to leave her eggs.

After about 30 days, the young owls hatch. The baby owls are covered with a coat of soft, white feathers.

When they are ten weeks old, owlets learn to fly. Six to nine months later, the young birds are fully grown and can leave their parents.

These great gray owlets will grow to be very big, just like their mother.

▼

OWLS AND HUMANS

Even though owls are protected by laws, they are in danger because of human habitats. When humans live close to nature, there is less space for owls and other animals. The pollution of the air and water are caused by humans. All of these things harm the habitats of Earth's animals.
Scientists are trying to solve these problems and protect animals and their habitats. But first people must learn to respect owls and their habitats. Humans can help keep owls from becoming **endangered** (en-DAYN-jerd) species.

WEB SITES:

You can learn more about owls on the Internet. Check out these Web sites:

http://theaviary.com/bd-040597.shtml

http://birding.miningco.com/

GLOSSARY

burrowing (BUR-oh-ing) Digging a hole in the ground for shelter.

camouflage (KA-muh-flaj) Markings on an animal's feathers, fur, or skin that help it blend into its surroundings.

climate (KLY-mit) The kind of weather a certain area has.

endangered (en-DAYN-jerd) When something is in danger of no longer existing.

habitat (HA-bih-tat) The surroundings where an animal lives.

mate (MAYT) A special joining of a male and female body. After mating, the female may have a baby or an egg grow inside her body.

migrate (MY-grayt) When large groups of animals or people move from one place to another.

nocturnal (nok-TER-nul) To be active during the night.

perch (PERCH) A tree branch or anything on which a bird can rest.

prairie (PRAYR-ee) A large area of flat land with grass but few or no trees.

predator (PREH-duh-ter) An animal that kills other animals for food.

prey (PRAY) An animal that is eaten by another animal.

rain forest (RAYN FOR-est) A very wet area that has many kinds of plants, trees, and animals.

rodent (ROH-dent) A kind of animal such as a mouse, a rat, or a squirrel.

saguaro (suh-GWAR-oh) A kind of huge cactus that grows in the desert.

species (SPEE-sheez) A group of animals that are very much alike.

talon (TA-lun) The long claws of an owl.

tundra (TUN-druh) The frozen land of the coldest parts of the world.

INDEX

A
Alaska, 11, 19
Antarctica, 4
Arctic, 11, 12

B
barn owls, 8
barns, 4, 6, 8
burrowing owls, 16

C
camouflage, 12
caves, 4
Central America, 16
climate, 11, 15

D
deserts, 4, 15, 19

E
eggs, 20
elf owls, 15
endangered, 22

F
feathers, 12, 16, 19, 20
forests, 4, 19

G
great horned owls, 19, 20

H
habitats, 4, 22

M
mating, 20
Mexico, 15
migrating, 4, 11

N
nesting, 4, 6, 8, 12, 15, 16, 19, 20
nocturnal, 6
North America, 4, 16

O
owlets, 19, 20–21

P
perch, 15
prairies, 4
predators, 12, 19
prey, 6, 12

R
rain forests, 19
rodents, 8, 12

S
saguaro cactus, 15
snowy owl, 11, 12
South America, 16, 19
species, 4, 22

T
talons, 6
trees, 4, 8, 15
tundra, 4, 11, 12

U
United States, 8, 15, 19